The Kingdom Promised

5/2010

Thank you! To J. M. Stockberger
I truly enjoy listening to you. You are a wonderful friend in Christ Jesus
Love,
Cary Hutchu

The Kingdom Promised

By
Carl J. Richter

 E-BookTime, LLC
Montgomery, Alabama

The Kingdom Promised

Copyright © 2010 by Carl J. Richter

All rights reserved. No part of this book may be reproduced or transmitted in any form or by any means, electronic or mechanical, including photocopying, recording, or by any information storage and retrieval system, without permission in writing from the copyright owner.

Library of Congress Control Number: 2010927374

ISBN: 978-1-60862-165-1

First Edition
Published April 2010
E-BookTime, LLC
6598 Pumpkin Road
Montgomery, AL 36108
www.e-booktime.com

Scripture quotations in this book are taken from the New King James Version Bible. 1983, 1975, 1971, 1966, 1965 & 1964 by Thomas Nelson, Inc.

Contents

Introduction	7
Acknowledgements	11
Everlasting Story	13
Our Creator God	14
God	19
The Soul	20
Religion	21
Heaven	24
The Son of God, Jesus	25
Jesus	28
Meditation	29
King of Kings	32
Out from Captivity	34
To the Nations	36
Pharaoh	40
Overcome Sin	41
Thinking of You	47
Mother	48
Memories and Miracles	49
Freedom	61
Death Caged	62
Satan	67
No Closed Doors	68
A Titanic Resurrection	69
Prayer for the Departed	73
On Board the Titanic	75
A Wonderful Promise	77

Tomorrow 83
Immortality 84
Heavenly Lights...87
Freedom, One Unity with God 88
The Spirit 90
Call to God You All the Earth 91

Introduction

Dear Brothers and Sisters,

What is our purpose? Allow me to speak in both present and of the future.

Indeed the family tree of life will soon be restored completely. You are complete in Him, who is the head of all principality and power. Being confident of this very thing, that He who has begun a good work in you will complete it until the day of Jesus Christ. *Colossians 2:10, Philippians 1:6.*

The joy of life and our existence is that we are all created by God through and by the word of our LORD Jesus. So, that we may live in unity, peace and love towards everyone especially those who may be our enemies. We live in the likeness of our heavenly Father, we live for each other, just like people who dwell in the same household together.

The earth is temporary. It is upon which we have learned as mortal flesh (human beings) good and evil, right and wrong, love, war and hate. Through all the corruption and perils of Satan (the devil) mankind, created by our eternal God has persevered, made possible through the living sacrifice and love of our LORD Jesus. Through Jesus Christ, we God's Children receive the promise of reconciliation and eternal salvation with God Himself.

We are one family in the spiritual sense, as we are in the physical. Soon we shall have a new heart and body, we will be the same yet spiritually immortal. We will never lose our memories, and our mind will function more fully and adequately.

It has been said by many, "This is only a vision of one's dream." We have seen or read the words of the Apostle John as described in the pages of the Bible of the past. This is of the future, the Apostle John seen the last day forthcoming. John then was told by God's angel to eat the words in which God spoke. That it would be sour in his stomach but in his mouth it would be as sweet as honey.

For one day, the day of the Lord will be at hand. There shall be no escape, only for the love within our heart and mind, empowered by God's grace. This is what keeps us from the unconsciousness of the 'grave,' forever. Though we may die, we will all be given life again!

We are indeed living human beings. First made mortal and one day soon shall be made immortal. We are all called God's children and one day we shall be heirs of God's Kingdom. We will dwell with our Lord God in His everlasting life with Him and Him with us. As it is written we will be under the grace and knowledge of our Father, forever and ever. Amen!

For our citizenship is in heaven from which we also eagerly wait for the Savior, Lord Jesus Christ, who will transform our lowly body that may be conformed to His glorious body. According to the working by which He is able even to subdue all things to Himself. (*Phil. 3*)

The following: The Kingdom Promised is an inspirational story. It interweaves ingredients of faith, hope and most importantly your purpose and God's Promise to all people. It's a refreshing outlook to life, in a revealing poetic sense into a descriptive narrative. This book offers the reader truth that God is real and how He reveals your purpose in life. It answers the question, "Can there really be peace in the entire world?", and retorts the question, "Will the world truly seek God collectively in Unity?"

Remember, dear brothers and sisters, everything comes about in due time. Pleasant words are like a honey comb, sweetness to the soul and health to the bones. (*Proverbs 16:24*)

Acknowledgements

It gives me great joy and honor to give all praise and glory to God, the creator of my life and in whom all things consist.

This book is dedicated to my wonderful wife, my angel on earth, whose love fills my heart with joy and song.

Dedicated to my parents whose instruction never wavered.

Dedicated to my mother whose love is of the Lord's and who taught me His love.

To my sister who lifts me up and wants the very best for me.

To my brother who gives me wisdom.

To my glorious nieces and nephew who show me what life is all about.

Everlasting Story

There is a familiar setting when were standing on unfamiliar ground. So much happening we want to find our place, looking towards new horizons we wander in open space. We hear many voices often not with godly sound, people listening but still earthly bound.

We search for answers continuing on our way yet still standing in fields of dirt and clay. God gives us the answers though somehow we break away.

The earth filled with beauty and glory and people we love and cherish. We stick to our guns battle hard everyday, War and Love, still we pray God don't let us perish.

We look, feel and taste what we believe to be good holding on to what we know, wavering in the sea like old rotten wood.

God embraces us all, leads us to His glory, it doesn't matter where we are or how far we drift away. We are all included in God's everlasting story.

Our Creator God

God is love. God has made the earth by his power, He has established the world by His wisdom, and has stretched out the heavens at His discretion. When He utters His voice, there is a noise of waters in the heavens: "And He causes the vapors to ascend from the ends of the earth. He makes lightning for the rain; He brings the wind out of His treasuries." *Jeremiah 10:12-13*

God created man in His own image; in the image of God He created him; male and female He created them. *Genesis 1:27*

Beloved, let us love one another, for love is of God; and everyone who loves is born of God and knows God. He who does not love does not know God, for God is love. In this the love of God was manifested toward us, that God has sent His only begotten Son into the world, that we might live through Him. In this love, not that we loved God, but that He loved us and sent His Son to be the propitiation for our sins. If God so loved us, we also ought to love one another. No one has seen God at any time. If we love one another, God abides in us, and His love has been perfected in us. By this we know that we abide in Him, and He in us, because He has given us of His spirit. *1 John 4:7-13*

Do not believe every spirit, but test the spirits, whether they are of God; because many false prophets have gone out into the world. By this you know the spirit of God: every spirit that confesses that Jesus Christ has come in the flesh is of God, and every spirit that does not confess that Jesus Christ has come in the flesh is not of God. *1 John 4:1*

"God is spirit and those who worship Him must worship in spirit and truth." The fruit of the spirit is love, joy, peace, longsuffering, kindness, goodness, faithfulness, gentleness and self-control. Against such there is no law. Those who are Christ's have crucified the flesh with passion and desires. If we live in the spirit, let us also walk in the spirit. Let us not become conceited, provoking one another, envying one another. *Galatians 5:22-26*

Do you not know that you are the temple of God and that the spirit of God dwells in you? *1 Corinthians 3:16* "Let the spirit of our eternal Father increase in you, filling your heart, mind and soul with God's love, grace and peace." Where your body is, let it stand on the solid foundation of God. *2 Timothy 2:19*

God is our refuge and strength, a very present help in trouble. Therefore we will not fear, though the earth be removed, and though mountains be carried into the heart of the sea; though its waters roar and be troubled, though the mountains shake with its swelling. There is a river whose streams shall make glad the city of God, the holy place of the dwelling places of the Most High. God is in the midst of her, she shall not be moved; God shall help her, just at the break of dawn. The nations raged, the kingdoms were moved; He uttered His voice, the earth melted. The Lord of hosts is with us; the God of Jacob is our refuge. Selah *Psalms 46:1-7* God who also has given us the spirit as a guarantee. *2 Corinthians 5:5*

The Mighty One, God the Lord, has spoken and called the earth from the rising of the sun to its going down. Therefore, since we are receiving a Kingdom which cannot be shaken, let us have grace, by which we may serve God acceptably with reverence and godly fear. For God is a consuming fire.

"God is not a man, that He should lie nor a son of man, that He should repent. Has He said and will He not do it? Or has He spoken and will He not make it good?" *Numbers 23:9*

Let the joy of the Lord fill your heart truefully and completely. Don't pretend to love God and to worship Him like the hypocrites. For it's not about being the smartest or speaking eloquent words. Believe in God truly, let Him into your heart; let God teach you. For God is not the author of confusion but of peace. *1 Corinthians 14:33*

In this manner, therefore pray: Our Father in heaven, hallowed be Your name. Your kingdom come, Your will be done on earth as it is in heaven. Give us this day our daily bread and forgive us our debts as we forgive our debtors. And do not lead us into temptation, but deliver us from the evil one. For Yours is the kingdom the power and the glory forever. Amen. *Matthew 6:8-13*

For us there is only one God, the Father, of who are all things, and we for Him; and one Lord Jesus Christ, through whom are all things and through whom we live. *1 Corinthians 8:6*

Then I looked, and behold, a whirlwind was coming out of the north, a great cloud with raging fire engulfing itself; and brightness was all around it and radiating out of its midst like the color of amber, out of the midst of the fire. Above the firmament over their heads was the likeness of a throne, in appearance of a sapphire stone; on the likeness of the throne was a likeness with the appearance of a man high above it. Also, from the appearance of His waist and upward I saw, as it were, the color of amber with the appearance of fire all around within it; and from the appearance of His waist and downward I saw, as it were, the appearance of fire with brightness all around. Like the appearance of a rainbow in a cloud on a rainy day, so was the appearance of the brightness all around it. This was the appearance of the likeness of the glory of the Lord. *Ezekiel 1:1-28*

For what if some did not believe? Will their unbelief make the faithfulness of God without effect? Certainly not! Indeed, let God be true but every man a liar. As it is written: "That you may be justified in your words, and may overcome when you are judged." *Romans 3:3-4*

Gracious is the Lord, and righteous; Yes, Our God is merciful. The Lord preserves the simple; I was brought low and He saved me. *Psalms 116:5-6*

Behold, God is my salvation, I will trust and not be afraid. *Isaiah 12:2*

Bless the Lord, O my soul, and forget not all His benefits: who forgives all your iniquities, who heals all your diseases , who redeems your life from destruction, who crowns you with loving kindness and tender mercies, who satisfies your mouth with good things, so that your youth is renewed like the eagle's. *Psalms 103:2-5*

God will wipe away every tear from their eyes; there shall be no more death, nor sorrow, nor crying; and there shall be no more pain, for the former things have passed away. God is the Alpha and the Omega, the Beginning and the End. *Revelation 21:1-7*

The tabernacle of God is with men, and He will dwell with them, and they shall be His people, and God Himself will be with them and be their God.

And they shall call His name Immanuel, which is translated, "God with us." *Matthew 1:23*

God

God the creator of everything, the Father of truth, of end and beginning. A living most divine being whose appearance far exceeds the universe, A God of compassion who created all birth whom as the word spoke created the earth.

God, the God of god's, there is none other, Who created your father, mother, sister and brother. God, who occupies all space, God of mercy and no one or nothing can take His place. His eyes are forever, His touch is gentle. His presence surrounds everyone and no one has ever seen His face!

God's love is spiritual though it resides within everyone. God's grace is everlasting, yet it cannot be bought, nor won! God's peace is abounding and continues throughout life. God is awesome with Him there is no strife!

God is giving He gives eternal living for those who repent of their ways and their sinning! God wants everyone to know if you choose His way you will spiritually grow. God says believe in His promise for it is very true, if you never deny Him you will one day see Him and He will see you!

The Soul

Your soul, consider it like a great house having such things inside providing comfort, security, nourishment, rest and solitude. Take the things out from the home and it soon becomes empty and void.

If what we desire shuts down, it becomes cold, empty, and without life, so is our soul. Take God out from it we have nothing, if you lose your faith and trust in Him we are alone, without hope.

Without God, who gives life and breath, WE; mankind would not exist. Without Jesus Christ, our Lord whom died so that we may have eternal life, who cleanses the soul and is forgiving of sins, our soul would be blotted out empty and we would have no part in the book of life.

Heaven is the great house we want to be part of; though we can't physically see heaven it exists! The Lord our God spoke a wonderful promise for those who repent and believe in Him and in Jesus Christ. We will be heirs and partakers of heaven, as His adopted children to dwell with God and Jesus Christ forever. AMEN!

Religion

"The world is the residence of one family. We are created by One God, through One voice; Jesus Christ."

Religion, pure religion is ordained by our God. It's having unification of Godly love towards everyone who has life. Not in sexual terms, like the world thinks. This becomes in some cases immoral and homosexual.

God taught His love and way of life to our first parents Adam and Eve. Adam and Eve disobeyed God and God drove them out of His Garden of Eden. God closed the doors so that no man could enter back in.

Several years afterward, religion became adequately ordained through God's son Jesus Christ. Jesus Christ, the living manifestation of God, God himself in the flesh. Jesus spoke and taught God's way of life to every person who lived and died!

It then came to be known as it is written, that God pre-ordained Jesus death. Jesus being without sin was found guilty to die on the cross and be crucified for all mankind to have eternal life! Jesus put sin to death, He overcome Satan the devil and his influence. Jesus died for all of mankind and for the sake of the world.

Our Lord Jesus opens our heart and our mind to let the Holy Spirit reside and live in us. God forgives us of our sins and remembers them no more. Through our faith in God and by the power and authority of our Lord Jesus Christ we can overcome sin and Satan.

Now we wait for the glory and appearance of our Lord and Savior, Jesus Christ. For Jesus will put Satan and his demons into the bottomless pit where he will be bound for one thousand years and deceive no one.

The death and resurrection of our Lord Jesus was ordained by God that mankind will be reconciled to God through Jesus Christ.

Within the mind of God is our state of being, our very existence and all who ever lived and died may live again. Just like our Lord and Savior Jesus Christ.

The love of God should be within our heart and mind, outpoured by our actions and way of life. Live in the likeness of Jesus Christ, in the likeness of God.

Through this way of living religions were formed to teach us the knowledge of God made possible through Jesus Christ.

Live the truth of God without un-godly rituals, live in hope and faith in God.

Religion in a sense of bodily exercise profits little but Godliness is profitable for all things. Having Promise of the life that now is and of that which is to come. *I Tim 4:6-16* and read: *James 1:21-27*

If anyone among you thinks he is religious and does not bridle his tongue but deceives his own heart this one's religion is useless.

Pure and undefiled religion before God and the Father is this: To visit orphans and the widows in their trouble and to keep one-self unspotted from the world.

Heaven

There's a Heaven, it sits beneath God's throne. God's kingdom prepared for us since birth. A kingdom that will generate overwhelming prosperity for everyone and heaven will be on earth!

There is a government which will unite everyone and the entire world will be at one. All the tears wiped away, no one will die and all animals will freely run!

There's a way which many will go, to always have hate and possessing no soul, who go on and on and think their in control.

Everyone knows God but many say they don't. There will be a few who live in the likeness of Jesus Christ, while many people won't!

In all these things God has given us our own voice, the right in making our own decisions. We call our freedom a choice!

There will come a day when this earth will pass away. God will create a new earth and all things will be new. God will create and everlasting government and Heaven will be with you!

The Son of God, Jesus

Before light existed, before emptiness had a name or time had a place and before the coming of ages; there was the Word, and the Word was with God, and the Word was God. Jesus was in the beginning with God. All things were made through Jesus and without him nothing would have been made. In Jesus was life and the life was the light of men. The light shines in the darkness and the darkness did not comprehend it.

There was a man sent from God whose name was John. This man came for a witness, to bare witness of the Light that all through Him might believe. He was not the Light but was sent to bare witness of that Light. That was the true Light which gives light to every man who comes into the world.

Jesus was in the world, and the world was made through Jesus and the world did not know Him. Jesus came unto His own and His own did not receive Him. As many who received Jesus, to them He gave the right to become children of God, even to those who believe in Jesus' name: Who were born, not of blood, nor of the will of the flesh, nor of the will of man, but of God. The Word became

Flesh and dwelt among us and we beheld His glory, the glory as of only begotten of the Father, full of grace and truth, Jesus.

John bore witness and cried out saying, "This was Jesus, of Whom I said, 'He who comes after me is preferred before me, for Jesus was before me.'" Of Jesus fullness we have all received, and grace for grace. For the Law was given through Moses but grace and the truth came through Jesus Christ.

No one has seen God at any time. The only begotten Son, Who was in the bosom of the Father, He has declared Him. Jesus came and taught the Word of God to the entire world. That all who heard His voice, may believe in His name. Repent and to reconcile to God; our only hope. Jesus, our LORD, God in the flesh taught us all things.

Jesus was invited into our homes ate and spoke among us. Jesus embraced everyone and instructed us all; yet we received Him not.

Jesus our Lord, Our Teacher, Our Brother and the only hope for peace and eternal life, died for our sins that men may receive the glory of God. Jesus was led like a sheep to be slaughtered, and was crucified. Beaten for our transgressions and defeated death, that death may have no hold on us and placed it on the cross. Jesus, by His death we are given hope of repentance. In reconciliation to our Creator and loving God, our Father we are forgiven. Jesus, by His life we are given the chance that we may have eternal life with Him, to become heirs and partakers in the Kingdom of God; to dwell with God and Jesus Christ forever with Him. Amen!

Jesus

When Jesus was born to us, He led many by the star, always near, but never too far.

Jesus came to us, 'Our Master and LORD,' our only King, the Son of God, who rules without a sword, yet many deceived Him, few worshiped and adored!

For this Our LORD mourns, for the many who call themselves worthy, but mock God daily. Remember? By His word all was born! Jesus is with us, He lives since the beginning, He's God's Son, who walks with us daily, yet our nations continue sinning!

Our LORD is preparing to be with us again, until then, never deny the LORD, and be a good citizen. Believe in Jesus, and remember His ways, for whom all souls He eases, give thanks to Him often, Our God, 'Our LORD Jesus.'

Meditation

Communication is an essential tool mankind has developed throughout generations. Communication helps get things done, it changes and develops societies, it defines cultures and a way of life and it writes laws. The way we communicate globally continues to change.

But when it comes to God, there are no special technical devices or methods in communicating with our eternal Father.

One way in communicating with our Father is through prayer, another is just as vital, meditation. Both are physical as well as spiritual. One might be while on our knees while the other might be our deepest thoughts or dreams while we are sleeping; this is normally called meditation. Remember God in your bed meditate on God in the night watches. *Psalms 63:6* Let's focus on Meditation.

How often do we listen to music? And what type of music do we listen to? Where do we go or what do we do throughout our daily routine that helps in dealing with the emotions or anxieties we face in our lives? What voices do we decide to hear in making the choices and decisions which challenge us each day? Is it your voice, your peers, friends or family? What motivates your character and your behavior?

Remember this prayer for inner peace: Search me O God, and know my heart; try me, and know my anxieties; and see if there is any wicked way in me, and lead me in the way everlasting. *Psalms 139:23-24*

Let not only your physical body and appearance be pleasing to God, but also your heart and your voice. Continue to grow in each new day to be pleasing in the eyes of the Lord our God. Let the words of your mouth and the meditation of your heart be acceptable in God's sight, the Lord of your strength and your redeemer. *Psalms 19:14*

Know this dear brothers and sisters: satan, the devil, the deceiver of all mankind premeditates mankind to die! To not have any part in God's kingdom and everlasting life. The devil premeditates daily on our death, he doesn't want any of mankind to experience the resurrection to eternal life! The devil desires all of mankind to premeditate and act on evil thoughts and desires on false beliefs and on what this world can offer you. Not in the promises of God and on his word not in Jesus Christ and what he has done for you nor in God's coming kingdom which you may be part of now! The devil wants you to experience pain, suffering and death, with no hope of salvation, or the resurrection Christ Jesus promises all of mankind. Satan wants mankind to live in the illusion that there is no life after death, that there is no resurrection of the body, and that Jesus Christ never existed!

Dear people mediate in the life and love of the Father, our eternal God. Strive for success in becoming ambassadors of Christ Jesus, Who spirit rest in all of Mankind and in whom all things consist. For it is written: "The Lord our God is always with you, he wants you to Meditate in him day and night and in his words which are written in the bible." *Joshua 1:9* His words and spirit is sealed in our hearts. Now He who establishes us with you in Christ, has anointed us in God who also has sealed us and given us the spirit in our hearts as a deposit.

Remember the words Jesus spoke when he said, "All things have been delivered to me by my Father, and no one knows who the son is but the Father, and who the Father is but the son and to whom the son wills to reveal him." And he turned to His disciples and said privately "Blessed are the eyes that see the things you see; For I tell you that many prophets and kings have desired to see what you see, and have yet not seen it and to hear what you hear and have not heard it." *Luke 10:22-24*

For Christ Jesus desires all men to be saved and to come to the knowledge of truth. For there is one God and one Mediator between God and men, Christ Jesus who gave Himself a ransom for all to be testified in due time. *I Timothy 2:4-6*

King of Kings

There are many things in this world that's pure, like gold, silver, and honey-bee nectar. There are pure ways of being a good listener and acknowledging those around you. There are many places and people the eye can see which proves this to be true.

 TAKE NOTICE WHILE ON YOUR JOURNEY, view that distance your eyes can't see, that pure way of life for eternity! Where brothers and sisters take the role of good listeners, truly loyal to friends and children of our mothers, to live in peace and happiness the way God uncovers!

 Through all the violence behold the dawning of a new day, for God will enrich you greater each day. No one shall take away your glory. Evil and violence will be cast away!

 Be strong through all the hate, put all your faith in God, put on the Lord's armor and foot-shod and behold the things the world has never seen, to Adam and Eve was only a dream. For you will inherit Gods kingdom everlasting, for those that have been dead are raised back to life! May the world come together and sing, to the Lord of Lords and King of Kings.

Out from Captivity

Thousands of years ago the Lord called out to those whom He had choose, men of great faith and they worshipped the Lord; the people knew God and God knew each one of them. God was with His people and He blessed and ordained leaders of His people and of nations; and Grace and peace was among God's people. It was by God's authority that His people were set free and by God's mercy led them out of captivity.

Then hardening of hearts began and set into the minds of God's people, who turned their back on God our creator; and the people began to worship idols, false teachers, greed and money; and over the course of generations walked back to the captivity that once bound them.

Now, today the Lord God calls His people, those who know good and evil, right from wrong and all who have walked in the path of the temptations of the earth to turn to God and repent. Whoever believes on Him will not be put to shame. For there is no distinction between Jew and Greek, for the same Lord over all is rich to all who call upon Him, for whoever calls upon the name of the Lord shall be saved. But, you, do not harden your heart for great is our Lord and mighty in power; His understanding is infinite. The Lord lifts up the humble; He casts the wicked down to the ground. Seek God in heart and mind, in character and well being; and you shall be heirs to God's everlasting life, a gift from God, made possible only through the love and grace of His son, Our Lord Jesus Christ whom brings the reconciliation of mankind to God and God to mankind. Amen.

To the Nations

All this is from God who reconciled us to Himself through Christ and gave nations the ministry of reconciliation: That God was reconciling the world to Himself in Christ not counting the nations sins against them. God has committed to the world the message of reconciliation. The nations, who reconcile themselves to God, are therefore Christ's ambassadors, as though God were making His appeal through you. To the world, her people and their nations, be reconciled to God. God made Jesus Christ who had no sin to be sin for you, so that in Him you might become the righteousness of God. The world knows the Lord can do all things; no plan of God can be thwarted (withheld from Him). "You said, 'listen now, and I will speak; I will question you, and you shall answer me! My ears have heard of you, but now my eyes have seen you; therefore I despise myself and repent in dust and ashes.'"

"In the last days, God says, 'I will pour out My Spirit on all people, the world and her nations. Your sons and daughters will prophesy, your young men will see vision and your old men will dream dreams. Even on My servants, both men and women, I will pour out My spirit and they will prophesy, for the day has come. I will show wonders in heaven above and signs on earth below, blood and fire and billows of smoke. The sun will be turned to darkness and the moon to blood before the coming of the great and glorious day of the Lord and everyone in the world who calls on the name of the Lord will be saved!'"

The Parable of the world, is a message from God, but woe to the nations and her people that dwell therein, who hears God's message about His coming Kingdom to be established on earth forever for who is lost and does not understand it, the evil one comes and snatches away what was sown in his heart.

To the world, nations and all her people, child of God, listen to this: Jesus of Nazareth was a man accredited by God to you by miracles, wonders and signs, which god did among you through Jesus Christ, and you yourself know. This man was handed over to you by God' set purpose and foreknowledge; and you, with the help of wicked nations in the world, put him to death by nailing Him to the cross but God raised Him from the dead, freeing Him from the agony of death because it was impossible for death to keep its hold on Him; and the world knows this about Jesus Christ: "You saw the Lord always before you. The Lord is at your right hand and the world's nations were not shaken.

Therefore the nations heart is glad and her peoples tongue rejoices; The worlds body will live in hope, because her nations will not be abandoned to the grave, nor will God let your Holy One, Jesus Christ see decay. God has made it known to all the world the paths of life; and her nations God will fill you with joy in His presence!

    The world's testimony was opened when Jesus Christ was resurrected, Jesus was not abandoned to the grave nor did His body see decay and the world and her nations are all witnesses of that truth. For that day, Jesus, exalted to the right hand of God, received from the Father the promise of the Holy Spirit, God poured out this which the world will now hear and see, and you will see in God's appointed time. "The nations and her people save yourself from your corrupt world, repent and be baptized every one of you, in the name of Jesus Christ for the forgiveness of sins and nations will receive the gift of the Holy Spirit. The promise is for all the world her nations and her children, all people on the earth, for all who are far off, and whom the Lord our God will call". God who made the world and everything in it is the Lord of heaven and earth, God does not live in temples built by hands and God is not served by human hands, as if He needed anything because He Himself gives all men life and breath and everything else. For all people God made the world, from one man God made every nation of men that one body of nations should inhabit the whole earth; and God determined the times set for them and exact places where they should live. God did this so nations would seek Him and perhaps reach out for Him and find Him, though he is not far from any nation. For in God the world lives and moves and we live and have our being. As some poet's have said, we are His offspring. "Therefore since we are God's offspring, we should not think that the divine being is like gold or silver or stone an image made by man's design and skill. In the past God overlooked such ignorance but know he commands the world, her nations and the people everywhere to repent. The nation in the world God loves, whom God loves and God rebukes and disciplines. God says to the world and her nations, 'Be earnest and repent. Jesus says, 'Here I am! I stand at the door and knock, will the world her nations hear My voice and open their hearts and minds; if anyone hears My voice and opens the door, I will come in and eat with him, as so a family sits together, and he with Me. Will the nations and her people overcome evil, I will give the right to sit with Me at My Fathers table, just as I, Jesus your Lord overcame and sat down with My Father on His throne'. 'Repent you the world and all her nations for the Kingdom of Heaven promised is near!'" Amen.

Pharaoh

The nations Leaders are like Pharaoh, his children are abandoned, women are raped, people are tortured under evil laws; and the road to peace is very narrow.

Many people of nations are lead to their slaughter, executed or stoned sister and brother. Walking passed children being taught by false teachers to hate and kill or take their own daughters, you're under the law and Satan's evil uncovered!

Education oppressed death undressed, God's law broken-up and digressed; your people run nowhere, your children obsessed.

While the evil one hides in mountains, caves, and rocks, his children are human shields and God's word ridiculed and mocked.

Woe! To Liars and hypocrites who pretend to know God, who causes violence and suffocation; and walks in the devil's foot-shod. For nations and Pharaoh are equal in part, both will thunder; and those who believe in God will have an everlasting new start!

Overcome Sin

Many of us have no problem admitting our faults to one another. We seek out answers or solutions to our problem, or bad habits, our desires or sins. So many of us find it so hard and in many ways not necessary to admit our sins or faults to God!

When we do wrong to our friends or family, generally.

Soon thereafter we apologize, it might be a day or two but we ask for forgiveness. We want the person to understand we didn't mean to hurt him/her and that we will do our very best not to make the same mistake again. This is what our living God, our heavenly Father desires of us. That we go to Him, seek Him out and to confess our sins, our faults or concerns to Him. God loves us and He truly wants us to call to Him in prayer and repent to Him our sins and to turn away from that which we know in our hearts is wrong.

God created you, He loves you very much and the love of His grace is always with you. For the day you turn to Him in prayer and forgiveness the Lord's Holy Spirit will abound in you and the process of reconciliation to God and you and you to God begins.

God calls you through the living word, through a friend or family member or through the Holy Spirit. God reaches out to us all through circumstances in our life. It starts with the choices we make, what we hear, feel and believe. However, God allows us to make decisions on our own; it's of our own free will to want to need or to believe in Him. God makes it possible for us to choose the choices we make; it's through His own authority. God made possible a wonderful promise between Him and mankind when He sent His only Son Jesus Christ our Savior into the world. No, there is no magic wand, no sorcery and it cannot be done through the tarot cards or psychic reading. True repentance begins from the heart. Know your sins. True forgiveness comes with the belief you know you are forgiven. Forgiveness is only possible through the grace of God. Believe in God and in Jesus Christ and you will be heirs in His everlasting Kingdom.

God created us to live with Him eternally. To worship Him always, believe in Him and in Jesus Christ, our Lord and Savior.

Remember, God does not want us to carry the 'mark' of sin that satan wants us to receive, satan tempts us to sin daily, he doesn't want us to have no part in eternal life with God. Satan doesn't have this choice and he wants to take us down with him.

If you are in sin, continue to cleanse yourself of it. Continue to repent, continue in prayer, meditation and fasting. Call on your friends and those you know can help you. Remember your Father in heaven and the words of Jesus who spoke: "Those who are first will be last and those who are last will be first." And of the worker, who started late yet received the same pay as the others who were early.

Remember this verse in *Hebrew 2:17-18* Therefore in all things. Jesus had to be made like His brethren, that He might be a merciful and faithful High Priest, in things pertaining to God. To make Propitiation for the sins of the people. For in that, He Himself has suffered, being tempted. He is able to aid those who are tempted.

If you truly believe in God and Jesus Christ continue in Faith. Remember your life is not your own but God's who created you.

For this reason give as Christ has given you, help those in need who desire as like Christ did, do the same.

The treasure you seek can only be found in Jesus Christ our Lord. God does so provide for all His children. So shall you do the same to those who find the Holy Spirit in you. Bring about the Lord's blessings on them; for He is gracious and a merciful God and His spirit rest in you. Do that which is pleasing in God's site and do not stray in the past. For we were all guilty of sin but press onward towards our Fathers will, for it is His will that all His children remain in Him.

All forms of sin indeed separate us from God. Most of us admit the wrongs which were done to us and how badly we've been mistreated by someone we loved or knew and in many cases by a stranger. These things can weigh us down throughout life and can cause us to do things to others or even to ourselves we wouldn't normally do. Whether, mentally or physically sin affects the mind, heart, and body. It can truly disrupt us throughout our daily life, sins such as; sexual immorality, prostitution, homosexual offenders, thieves, the greedy, drunkards, swindlers, idolaters, adulterers, and the wicked. *I Cor. 6:9* Also: Obscenity, foolish talk, coarse jesting. *Eph. 5:4* And; Hatred, Jealousy, fits of rage, selfish ambition, witchcraft, debauchery, orgies, envy, factions, discord, impurity and dissensions. *Gal. 5:19* If you are mentioned in any of these sins here is a prayer for you. "Today, my life is in Your hands O Lord my God, as it always was; and will always be. I heard the voice of God spiritually within, He called me. Forgive me of my sins O God, lay Your loving hands upon me and cleanse my soul so that You may call me Your child. Cleanse my heart, my mind and my thoughts God for I have acted foolishly in your site. I have given myself over to the cares of this world and have corrupted Your temple, the body and life You gave to me O God. For You are a merciful God, Father of life and of death, pure, just as You O

God. I repent from my sins O God and believe in the name of Jesus Christ who takes away the sins of the world. Who is the life, and the light over all creation. You, O Lord sanctify the body, the heart and mind. Sanctify me O Lord and present me holy in Your sight." Amen.

Please read with me in *Colossians 1:21-22.* Once you were alienated from God and were enemies in your minds because of your evil behavior. Now God has reconciled you by Christ's physical body through death to present you holy in His sight, without blemish and free from accusation, if you continue in your faith, established and firm, not moved from the hope held out in the gospel. The gospel you have heard and which was proclaimed to every creature under heaven. Also, in *Ephesians 2:12-13* remember the time we were once separate from Christ Jesus excluded from citizenship in Israel and foreigners to the covenants of promise, without hope and without God in the world. Now in Christ Jesus you who once were far away have been brought near through the blood of Christ.

Do not receive God's grace in vain, For He says, "In the time of My favor I heard you and in the day of salvation I helped you." *2 Corinthians 6:2*

We can name many blessings we are given, but never likely to remember them all. Many of us have been saved from possible death but can we recall all the people who had a hand or took time in saving us?

Remember, when anger or depression sets into your very heart and mind or if you feel vulnerable to temptation in making a decision which may affect your life, trust in the Lord your God and seek Him for answers, will you?

I leave with you a glorious understanding of God's Love. Before time existed, before the void was filled and before mankind was given breath, God had reconciled His life to you. God has indeed already forgiven you.

Thinking of You

You are a wonderful blessing of hope and love. Living beyond the scope of self is a hard choice. And caring or fulfilling the needs of others around you to ensure the well being of others especially the children is a daily choice, a sacrifice.

Your life goes far and beyond yourself, most times Life's trials tackle your decision to continue in faith and love; and I pray everyday for you to God in heaven above to surround your well being with peace, comfort, solitude and love.

You are not ever alone, dig deep down within and search your heart; believe God is with you even in your dark place or your very own home. If anger or depression sets in your heart and well being, trust in the Lord; for knowing is believing. God's spirit is with you through our Lord Jesus, your helper who never rests. And your life will be fulfilled in this life and in the next. Amen

Mother

You ever stop to notice what life itself brings? You ever stop to embrace children, those you love, animals and such things? Do you believe you are part of something holy and true? Someone to love, honor and respect. Enjoy life and what life brings: not corrupted, manipulated, nor clouded by rings.

Do you know the elderly, the old, the wise, and the meek, Children, fathers, mothers and the weak; is part of one God we should all seek.

Do you believe truth unadulterated by lies? Does your character define your appearance as time passes by? For even in darkness I'll be by your side. Like words to a story from one to another: 'Believe in God, and cherish your MOTHER.'

Memories and Miracles

I was born August ninth, nineteen sixty seven in the city of Buffalo, New York. My memory of my life dates as early as 1972, the year I began kindergarten. I was one of three children; I have a sister and a brother. My parents were both Catholic, so their choice was to enroll us in a catholic school. Our parents always taught us about God and simply put, God was our everyday conversation. Both in school and out of school it was, God is the essential part of our lives. Little by little God became more present, while the world I grew up in became less and less noticeable. I truly believed everyone in the world grew up believing God or at least knew a life similar to mine.

    At an early age I believed in God, even though I couldn't see him. Even then I somehow knew something or someone very great made me. I remember telling my classmates or just anyone in particular, God made you, you're awesome! Looking back most people would say you were naive and unless you start learning about the World you live in it will consume you.

Maybe I wasn't naive but I didn't know how cruel the world would be, really, who does at a young age?

My memory dates back to my first confession: an acknowledgement of guilt. While in the confessional: a place where a priest hears your confessions, I began to tell the person on the other side my sins I had committed earlier that week. I didn't quite understand what sins I have caused I explained but that I had a question. Then, a voice on the other side said: "Confess to your father your question." I didn't understand his question either, so I continued. "Sir, do you want me to go home and ask my dad or would you like me to ask God my question?" The voice on the other side explained. "Tell father Bob your question and I shall answer you." I would say I was rather confused so I began to ask, "Bob, I only have two fathers, the one here on earth and the one I pray to in heaven, Your not my dad, so are you who I pray to in heaven? "Soon after the door to my part of the confessional opened, then the man in the robe shouted, "Get out! Go sit over there," he pointed, "and do one hundred Hail Marys, I'll deal with you later." This was only the beginning of things which happened to me. That either changed the way I thought about people or prolonged my life on earth anyway it had a profound affect on my life.

Two weeks had past since my ordeal in the confessional, in late November of 1972. It was very cold out that day and there was a lot of snow on the ground. Usually if our class was in good behavior, our teacher would let us children play outside and today was no different. We couldn't wait to go outside and play in the snow. We were asked by our teacher to work together to make a snowman and that's exactly what we began to do, most of us. Some of us started snow fights, while others made snow angels or done anything else just to stay warm, or try to anyway.

    I was part of the snow fight and we were having a blast. Bobby took a direct hit in the face, he just laughed and retaliated. Jimmy received a series of hits to the head, his stomach and two in the back. This fight was just heating up! Until, soon after Jimmy received his hits He wanted to retaliate on someone, anyone! Jimmy picked me and I was ready for the challenge. I threw first hit Jimmy right in the gut. Then Jimmy gathered up a big chunk of snow and came charging after me. Jimmy got me in the back with a snowball and followed up with pushing me in the snow. We were all laughing when I stood up someone yelled, "Look at his hands, they look like ice cubes." That's when I looked at my hands. He was right! My hands were completely covered with ice! I tried biting the ice off my fingers but it wouldn't work. Without delay, I ran home as fast as I could, only to stop briefly at the traffic light, where Mrs. Francis, the crossing guard signaled clear for us kids to cross. I lived across the street from the school I attended, thank God! When Mrs. Francis seen my hands she shouted, "Go home as quickly as you can, I hope your hands will be alright?"

No sooner did I cross the street a great big dog attacked me, but even that dog couldn't bite the ice off my hands! (I even think back today, was that a miracle?) When I got home I smelled delicious pies or something that good baking in the oven. My dad preparing the doe for another one. My dad was amazed at the sight of my hands and directed me over to the space heater. "Here" he said softly. "Keep your hands this high until the ice is off your hands, okay, don't worry son you'll be alright."

I don't remember how long it was but slowly the ice began to melt then I was able to move my fingers and feel them too! "This is great!" I shouted and I kept on thanking God and my dad. Then my dad hugged me and I was so happy as if it never happened. My dad said, "Let's go have some apple pie."

I remember that same year, it was before Christmas. My mother took my sister, baby brother, who was in a stroller and me for a walk. When we approached an overpass I heard a familiar voice calling my name, my mom was holding my hand. It was Michael! He wanted me to go to the playground with him, which was across the street. At moments notice I pulled my hand from my moms grip and ran across the street towards my friend Michael. I never made it across the street. Suddenly, I heard a loud noise, the kind you would hear if someone slammed on their car brakes and tires locking up, skidding on the road. Instantly, I was under a car. I heard my mother screaming, "OH NO!" I heard crying and my ears began to ring. I stayed where I was and notice the car I was under backing up slowly. Soon I was able to move freely and tried to get to my feet but a man would not let me. He was crying and said, O dear God I'm sorry." That's when I began to cry and I cried for a long time. The man picked me up and placed me gently in his car, my mom, sister and brother were in the car as well. Suddenly we arrived at the hospital. Soon I was in this machine covering my entire body. I was scared and crying. My mom was holding my hand, this time I didn't ever want to let go. The more someone tried moving my hand the louder I began to cry. I have never been so scared in my life. Not so long after, I was lying in a hospital bed. A man dressed in white approached me. "I am a doctor," he said. The car could have taken your life and you wouldn't have seen your family again. Do you understand what happened?" the doctor asked. I said, "I pulled away from my mothers hand and I think I got hit by a car?" The doctor replied, "You came very close to losing your life, that car could have killed you! You managed to escape without a scratch. This is a miracle from God that nothing happened to you!" The doctor continued, "Don't ever disobey your parents again and more importantly never pull your hand away from them." I said, "I'll never do that again, I promise!"

I'll never forget that day on my ninth birthday. We had recently moved from across the street of my school to several blocks down the road, still relatively near by our school. It was early morning, and when I set my mind to something this important I usually wake up earlier than anyone in the house. So, I am talking early! I got on my bike and headed towards my grandfathers house.

Grandpa knew I was coming to visit him, so did my parents.

Grandpa lived across and down the street from our School and away I went. I was pretty much in a hurry. Although, my parents always instructed me to walk my bike across the street, I decided I would stay alert of traffic lights and only stop if necessary! I was getting closer but still a few blocks away. I was approaching the Laundromat where my grandpa often went. I was nearing a traffic light at the intersection. My light was green, so I proceeded. The next thing I saw was a bright red car roaring fast at me, all I could do was take impact. I flew over the car that hit me, (I noticed it was a convertible), and onto the hood of the car behind. I didn't make it to grandpa's house. My bike was totaled. My lip was bleeding but, worse of all the same man (priest) whom listened to my confession was the same person who hit me! I was completely devastated and shocked! Not to mention I had to hear priest Bob blame me for the accident. Priest Bob threw my bike into the trunk of the car. He gave me a hanky for my bloody lip and said, "I am going to take you home to your parents." Soon I was home; mom greeted us at the door. Priest Bob said, "Here's your son, teach your son to obey traffic signals, he's alright, have a nice day." Then Priest Bob left.

I remember having been in at least ten similar bike accidents not once have I spent any time in a hospital, or had any broken bones to mention!

One day, my friends and I went out to play at the train tracks. We approached a train that was still, it just wasn't moving. So, I decided to climb inside one of its box cars, the door was slightly open. When I got in I shut the door, my friends outside helped me. I tried getting out after a little while but the door wouldn't open, it was too hard. I was yelling, "Let me out! Let me out!" My friends couldn't help me either. One of them ran to my house to get my dad, he came and let me out. Thank God! Eleven times over and over! My 15th birthday, I was at my younger brothers little league baseball championship game his team won. He had two, two base hits, three runs batted in and two home runs! When the game was over my parents surprised me with a birthday party! Many of my family and friends were there as well. I had cake and opened gifts! Then, I opened a card, most everyone was busy talking or joking. In the card I discovered fifteen dollars and a rolled marijuana joint ready for smoking. I knew some people who smoked marijuana and some who sold it; my friends mostly.

Later that day, I made a decision to smoke the joint, (marijuana). It went straight to my head and made me somewhat dizzy. I felt different, perhaps, I even talked different. Some people noticed as well. They didn't know it was marijuana but only believed I was sick.

Ten years had passed-by and I was still smoking marijuana. Mostly, I would smoke by myself, sometimes, not often; I'd smoke with my cousin. I never wanted to influence anyone else.

I also tried coke, acid, mushrooms, rush and smoked crack, once we smoked an entire cookie in a day. The Lord was still by my side though all my sins. These things I done could have killed me, I could have remained addicted to them. Like so many people before me but I never was. Most all these drugs I walked away from except, marijuana. It still had its hold on me. I remember times I'd smoke an ounce of marijuana in a day or two. Most of the time I was at home in my room with the door locked, with as much marijuana as I could afford, sometimes alcohol. Like so many other times before, I'd take my fathers gun, a 357 magnum, I played Russian roulette a few times. All the while God was with me, the fact is and apparent, I was still alive.

Years had passed by so quickly since the day I stopped smoking marijuana or taking drugs altogether. In that moment I didn't fully understand why, I just knew.

However, I still drank heavy at times, sometimes even more. It was mid 2002; March I believe, I was in my room, the door was locked and I was drinking alcohol. I began to read the Bible, looking for me inside its pages, a reflection of the person I am, looking for my identity.

Maybe I was looking for God; perhaps he would wake me up with His Words. I remember praying. "Dear God", I began. "You know me God, I'm nothing and I know I am not pleasing in Your eyes. How can You walk with me when I continue to drift from Your side? Pull away from Your hand? I am ashamed dear God! I'm not worthy of Your word, not worthy to be created and certainly not worthy to receive Your promise!" I took another glass of alcohol and loaded the 357 magnum, it was a six-shooter. I put three bullets in the chamber, locked it quickly, put the gun to my head and pulled the trigger. I quickly repeated. I opened the chamber, re-positioned the bullets in the chamber, locked it quickly and put the gun to my head. This time I didn't pull the trigger. I tried again and still I did not pull the trigger. What's wrong? I questioned. "If there is a bullet in the barrel I'd be dead now!" I slowly eased the gun from my head, pointed towards the ceiling and fired! A bullet shot out from the gun, through the ceiling and rest in one of the rafters in the attic.

I came close many times before believing that I was on the path of healing. That I prayed and studied often enough God's Spirit would direct me in the way that I should go. How many times I did not understand God's Love, His grace and Spirit was with me every single day, all the time. One day I am so close to God, to find myself drifting away with the world the next.

At times I often think back on the day I ran across the street and consider the more I take life for granted, the more I lose sight of God's grace.

Thirteen years ago I met a young woman during an eight day church holy festival in Niagara Falls, New York; ten thousand people were in number. As I exited the convention center lobby I glanced over my right shoulder and seen her. She was beautiful! She had strawberry blonde hair and was wearing a red dress. Time stopped for a moment, I had to catch my breath. I said to her, "I've seen you before, I remember one year you sang The Rose, during a talent contest. You had a white dress on and you were holding roses. I took a picture of you that day and I'll bet my mother has your picture in her purse."

I often prayed to God, that one day He would find me a woman that I would marry. Not just any woman, one that would be considered heavenly, like an angel on earth. We talked for a long time that day. We had also walked by the falls, where she sang me a song. We held hands and I respected her. We started dating and writing each other often. We were falling in love and marriage was in our hearts. Many times I would explain to her that I was not good enough for her, she could find someone else who's better than me. In the end I told her, I can't do this. She told me, "Your running away from what you know in your heart is right! I can see it in your eyes you're afraid because you are a coward! You're pulling away from me just like you pulled away from God." I should have realized the bad decision I made. "Why do I keep slamming my life and pushing the people I love away?" We went our separate ways that day.

Thirteen years and one week had passed by since I turned away the woman of my prayers. Four days ago I could have killed myself; my mother has the bullet I pried out from the attic rafters.

My cousin, my brother and I had just got home from work. We were partners in Home Improvement. We walked in hearing the phone ringing. I answered it and as soon as I heard the voice on the other side, I knew who it was! It was the woman I walked away from thirteen years ago. She called to tell me she had a dream that I was in trouble, that she still loves me and that she had been with me since the day we first met. Somehow time and the grace of God's love brought us together again. Not too long after we got married. All Praise belongs to God.

Jesus, Our Lord and Savior loves us all! I truly know. The Lord is with you everyday of your life and miracles are His divine gift.

Almost all of us have a story to tell when our lives almost took a tragic end. We came close many times in making good decisions, to see we failed because we made the wrong choice. Some of us remain in this loop and were eager to point fingers or pass judgment on someone or something that caused us to make wrong decisions. One thing I truly know, once you let God's love, grace and spirit in your heart and mind, you will begin to heal physically and spiritually.

I truly am healing with God's Spirit. Perhaps I should have started a while back. Maybe I refused to let God's Spirit in enough to allow His spirit to heal me in years past. I didn't except God's grace or mercy and certainly didn't expect it.

Sometimes in so many cases like mine, and there are many of us out there, it often does take severe moments or miracles that show or tells us God's Spirit was always there to begin with, to recognize how often we reject it.

Freedom

What is to live in peace and happiness? To worship our LORD Jesus, whom many never saw .follow the commandments of God, that's the law. Put away corruption, the evil which can snare many hearts and all nations. Remember Sodom, Edom, and the Holocaust? Put away hate and everyone will have FREEDOM!

In this world, the road to FREEDOM is to many like a land closed off, 'No one can enter!' All want FREEDOM, but most all are pretenders.

When has our world come together under One God? Who created all things and created you, and for you life He brings! What nation has not killed since the beginning, or who can say who lives, and does not continue sinning? Though clues to our woes persist, are nations are sadly amiss. God, we sure need Him! Let's come together, and pray for true FREEDOM!

Death Caged

His name is Lucifer, who was prince of the air, the morning star. That ancient serpent called the devil, who leads the whole world astray. He was hurled to the earth and his angels with him. Satan was cast down from heaven by the authority of God and is held out by God's angels. Satan is known as death and the accuser of all mankind.

Satan wants all of mankind to die a death known throughout the generations. To be thrown into the lake of fire and burning sulpher. For this is Satan's future the end of life and freedom.

The Lord God formed man out from the dust of the ground and breathed into his nostrils the breath of life and man became a living being. Then, the Lord God caused a deep sleep to fall on the man, who was named Adam, and he slept. God took one of his ribs and closed up the flesh in its place. Then the rib which the Lord God had taken from man He made into a woman and He brought her to the man, and Adam said: "This is now bone of my bones and flesh of my flesh, she shall be called woman, because she was taken out of man," soon after temptation fell on man. Lucifer, in the form of a serpent who is satan the deceiver; deceived the woman to eat from the tree of which God commanded you should not eat. She also gave some to her husband and he ate. Then the Lord God greatly multiplied the sorrow and conception of the woman; and said to man: "Cursed is the ground for your sake; in toil you shall eat of it all the days of your life," and said also, "For dust you are and to dust you shall return."

A time had passed when God sent His only begotten son into the world, Jesus Christ. That through Jesus all may receive the gift of grace and truth. Through Jesus Christ all may receive the gift of His promise to receive immortality and to be adopted sons and daughters of God the Father and to dwell in His everlasting Kingdom forever!

In *Ephesians 2:12-13* it says; remember the time you were once separate from Christ Jesus, excluded from citizenship in Israel and foreigners to the covenants of promise, without hope and without God in the world. Now In Christ Jesus you who once were far away have been brought near through the Blood of Christ.

Believe and trust in the Lord for satan will never receive the promise of God. Satan is loose only by the authority of God. And in a time satan, Lucifer the devil will be thrown into the lake of fire and burning sulpher. Lucifer indeed was created immortal from the beginning. But mankind was created mortal, flesh and human of the dust of the ground. God created mankind to choose immortality, to believe right not wrong, to love not hate, to believe in the promise of God through Christ Jesus. For God wants us to go and sin no more once we make the choice to repent to Him and ask God for forgiveness.

God in His gracious love wants us all to dwell with Him and in Jesus Christ Forever. Don't waste this wonderful promise of God, to reject His love; don't waste life to become dust forever! Satan doesn't have the choice!

Soon, in a time satan will be bound by the authority and chains of God. No longer free to move about and held in place forever. Satan will be in a place unable to move, unable to leave and he will see nothing with his eyes. Satan's spirit will be held in one place kept in chains, unable to speak or whisper to anyone, unable to neither deceive nor confuse mankind especially the children. Satan's voice no longer heard or felt and his demons will also be burned and gone forever. Satan's powers will never work nor will be felt by mankind again. Satan's actions will no longer progress, his ways and evil deceptions will be forgotten and dead, in the lake of fire and burning sulphers. This is the future satan wants all of mankind to suffer with him, the future satan knows he can't escape from.

But, after a time, for a little while satan will be loose by the authority of God, as it is written. And satan will gather an army to try to crush the camp of God and his people. Then, the Lord God will bind satan with chains. And no more will he ever be loose, but will burn for eternity in the lake of fire and burning sulpher. Inside satan will always be dead, his whispers and words will attack him. When satan moves he will be in great pain for what he has done to God's people. Satan will crumble into ashes and awake again in pain. Satan will be bound forever and for all eternity, dead and gone forever!

For this very reason satan wants all of mankind to die, to reject God and to never come to know Jesus Christ. Satan does not want mankind to believe in Jesus Christ and God our Father. Satan wants your soul to be cast away, blotted out of the book of life and gone forever with him.

God promises mankind a wonderful gift a beautiful life long after you awake from your grave. To a life eternal, an immortal life! God wants you to dwell in a land filled with milk and honey, with God the eternal Father and Jesus Christ, His Son.

Remember this reading in *Jeremiah 31:34*; no longer will a man teach his neighbor or man his brother, saying "Know the Lord", because they will all know Me from the least of them to the greatest, "For I will forgive their wickedness and will remember their sins no more."

"Don't be caught by the snares nor deceptions of satan, turn from evil and do what is good, seek peace and pursue it earnestly." 'Believe in God and Christ Jesus our Lord, and repent from sin. Be good to everyone, treat all people as you yourself want to be treated.' 'For you will be part of God's everlasting Kingdom; a place where satan has no home, a Kingdom where satan has no name!"

Satan

Satan is much like the earth, though possessing beauty, grows evil since birth. The earth is Satan's land of sorrow, mixed with love and hate, killing and shame blended-in for tomorrow, and what does he create?

In the time Satan has left, he wants to rule, make nations his slaves, and earth is dying, lands filled with tombstones and graves! Beware! Satan the deceiver is upon the earth, an image in many ways, his kings of many faces. To those who deny God, destroy freedom, and profane the way of life, you will be put in your places!

Satan and the earth are equal in part, for both will thunder. Many people will turn to God and witness the earth and Satan torn-up apart, where then, will be your heart!

No Closed Doors

We are to believe that everyone on earth has peace? Then afflicting pain upon the innocence, children left and abandoned, many making choices on whether to abort them, then hide behind closed doors.

The people do the same to themselves, through pain and suffering many separate, the dinner table is empty, God is far away; it seems we have put the way of good living upon highest shelves.

People become bored, many become scorned, many are laid to waste without being warned. Different voices, deceptions, and many corridors; the world's winds are opened, there are no closed doors!

Speaking of our time here to serve, never once our life we deserved. God's voice, to many is mocked; hidden behind their false identity, God's truth is sealed and locked.

Our time we have left? It was never to be mocked; God holds the key to our life's plot, soon your closed doors will be unlocked!

A Titanic Resurrection

A time, and a time after, Our God created the earth and all that's upon the earth, and all that's in the earth, the abyss and far beyond. He set the heavens, waters, atmosphere, and space apart; affixed time and space, day and night.

God created all things in heaven and on earth, the universe and beyond, He set the stars in place, the planets, the moons and the suns. God created mankind, both male and female.

All that God created, creatures, animals of all kinds, birds, fish, and everything that can and cannot be seen and all the things yet to be created, born or made for its place and time. After all that God had created He saw that it was good and blessed it with His Love and Grace.

Then, temptation struck hard at the very heart of mankind. They took to themselves the prerogative of deciding what is good and what is evil, they, we the people rejected God. And, God saw man growing wise in his own knowledge and understanding; and did things displeasing to God.

Soon followed murders, sacrifices of men, women and children, terrible hateful crimes, ethnic cleansing; wars and bloodshed. And, the voice of those murdered and slain cries out to God from the ground and from the waters.

And so, the Lord looks around upon the earth with anger; grieved by the hardness of hearts. And the earth, yet still corrupt before God and the earth yet still filled with violence. But, through the love, life and grace of our Lord and Savior, Jesus Christ, we are saved, our only hope. And the promise made certain to us, 'The Lord knows those who are His, and all who believe in Jesus Christ will for sure see Him face to face in the glory of His Holy Kingdom.

The Lord helps His troubled people from the many who rise up against them. And there are many who say there is no help for you in God. But God is our shield, our glory, the one who lifts up our head. We cry out to the Lord with our voice and He hears us from His holy hill.

In a time, disaster shall go forth from nation to nation, a great whirlwind shall be raised up from the farthest parts of the earth, and they will say "wail, shepherds and cry! Roll about into ashes you leaders of the flock for the days of your slaughter and your dispersions are fulfilled; you shall fall like a precious vessel.

But we have this treasure in earthen vessels that the excellence of the power may be of God and not of us. We are hard pressed on every side, yet not crushed; we are perplexed but not in despair;

persecuted but not forsaken; struck down but not destroyed. Always carrying about in the body the dying of the Lord Jesus, that the life of Jesus also may be manifested in our body, for we who live are always delivered to death for Jesus sake, that the life of Jesus also may be manifested in our mortal flesh, so then death is working in us, but life in you.

Then we will see a great white throne and He who sits on it, from whose face the earth and the heaven fled away. And there was found no place for them. And the dead, small and great will stand before God and books will be opened and the dead will be judged according to their works, by the things written in the books. And the sea will give up the dead who were in it and death and Hades delivered up the dead who were in them. And they will be judged each one according to his works. And death and Hades will be cast into the lake of fire.

Then we will see a new heaven and a new earth, for the first heaven and the first earth had passed away, also there will be no more sea, for the tabernacle of God will be with men and He will dwell with them and they shall be His people and God Himself will be with them and be their God. He who overcomes shall inherit all things and I will be his God and he shall be My son.

Remember this prayer in your thoughts: *Psalms 51:9-12* Hide your face from my sins and blot out all my iniquity, create in me a pure heart, O God and renew a steadfast spirit in me. Do not cast me from Your presence or take Your Holy Spirit from me. Restore to me the joy of Your salvation and grant me a willing spirit, to sustain me. Then I will teach transgressors Your ways and sinners will turn back to You.

Prayer for the Departed

For the ones who have passed away and for those who yet shall, I will not speak of their past. For anyone who has known him or her has a personal account or testimony. I would rather speak of the future and in prayer.

May God fill your heart and mind with His divine spirit, restore your soul and clothe your body with His grace. When you awake from your sleep, may you know and believe in Him whom has resurrected you from death to life, who has indeed created you and of whom you stand before, the Father of eternal life, our LORD God almighty. AMEN

May the voice of those who love you, who stood by your side in sickness and in health, those who love the Father, people of God whom the Lord will not forget remain in you, may the stillness of their love stay with you. May your heart and mind receive the voice of God and welcome His presence. Receive the fullness of God's grace restored completely to the fullness of His glory;

forgiven, reconciled and received into the everlasting peace of God's wonderful life. AMEN

On Board the Titanic

"All Aboard!" On board the Titanic is much like the Earth, surrounded by its governments and politics, many become sick.

On board the Titanic, you may attend church or arrange meetings to become strong; while others fight and dictate and don't get along.

On board the Titanic, you're invited to parties, dances, lectures, and games; some to busy in their fortunes and fame,

On board the Titanic, you can buy or trade and gain a lot on things you have made.

On board the Titanic, you'll be locked up, held, or caged, like prison camp slaves, you're along for the ride; you have no say.

On board the Titanic, you might beware, you may be killed or commit suicide; and no one will care.

On board the Titanic will come a surprise! When it crashes and sinks before your eyes; then you'll hear the people mourn, "We'll all perish, as we have been warned!"

The Earth and the Titanic are equal in part, for she will thunder; and you, who want to be saved? It's within your heart.

A Wonderful Promise

I am sure some of us have thought what it would be like to go back in time or perhaps change time. But you already have the choice to change time, to make tomorrow better and to change or overcome what you've done today.

Maybe you are saying; "No, I cannot make tomorrow better and certainly can't change time!"

No one can control life or death nor can anyone control the things other people do. And remember your life is not yours but the Lords. And everyone everyday is left with daily choices and decisions. Yet good or evil decisions will be made.

In your life has anxiety overwhelmed you? Has the care of this world effected your decisions you've made? Has the loss of a loved one changed your outlook on life? Does fear trouble your heart and mind? Are you surrounded by terror, destruction, ethnic cleansing, murder, suicide bombings or disease? Has substance abuse taken over your life? Are you a gang member? Have you murdered anyone? Or have you beaten or raped anyone? Are you a fornicator, molester, do you masturbate? Do you think bad thoughts and hate? Do you or have you acted on these things? More importantly were you a victim or hurt by such sins?

In certain these things, not to hurt or accuse you, for I am a sinner; but to give you rest with this promise: "Your body can be broken down by the men of the world, but with God's Spirit in you, you are saved and have life through Jesus Christ who died for you." *Job 17:1-11* and know this, yet while we were still sinners Christ Jesus died for us. Our sins were hung on the cross with Jesus, who gave Himself over to those who killed Him; so that by His death our sins would be removed from us. Our sins forgiven, forgotten by the Grace of God and we are raised up with Christ whom God raised Himself from the grave; for Jesus Christ conquered death, He is eternal; He is our Lord and Savior. Therefore, we make it our aim, whether present or absent to be well pleasing to Him. *2 Corinthians 5:9*

Even if you don't know God or think that you are far removed from His presence, God is never absent from you. God gives us His Spirit, He gives us His Grace, God sent us Jesus Christ; His only begotten Son, who makes possible eternal life. All this God gives us before we ever knew Him, before we ever asked. Yet, by the Grace of God's love He forgives us our sins and leads us not into temptation but delivers us from the evil one. And sinners were we all, but were washed, set apart and justified in the name of the Lord Jesus and by the Spirit of our God. *I Corinthians 6:11*

So how can we change time? Make tomorrow better? And change what we have done today? By asking God to forgive us our sins and by asking God to our enemies who have hurt us, Believe God will heal you. God is in charge, He is the creator of life. By asking God through Jesus Christ to sanctify you with His Holy spirit, for Jesus is our Savior.

Consider the world in which we live. This world is ruled mostly by hate, greed, lust, envy, malice, deceit, and hypocrisy. Yet, we all strive to get along. No matter how much men break down the body of the people; still many raise up in unity declaring the glory of God. No matter how much murder or the punishment men afflict on the body, still many stand in Victory giving thanks and glory to God! No matter how much hate we see or witness in the world, still many more continue to live in peace giving glory to God, for each new day of life.

If God is not the creator of life, and everything seen and unseen, if God does not exist, mortality would not exist in this world. In fact, we would not exist and I would not be writing to you today. Why would I? If God don't exist, why would I have love for you? Why would you have love for anyone? Believe this fact, God is Love, Satan is hate! God is Holy, Satan is evil! God is omnipotent, (almighty having unlimited authority), God is Omniscient, (having infinite awareness, understanding and insight). God forgives sinners and His promise is sure! God was, is and yet always will be and God has no successor! Now, Satan exalts himself above all that is called God or that is worshipped so that he sits as God in the temple of God, showing himself that he is a god. Satan is the devil, slanderer, supreme spirit of evil, demon, a wicked person; Satan is the great dragon, the serpent of old that deceives the whole world. Satan is the beast who hates mankind and Satan blasphemies against God, and Satan is the great tempter who tempts the whole world to sin.

Do not let your heart be troubled, Satan exists! And Satan wants all that God created; Satan wants all of mankind to die! He possesses the earth, he and his demons.

There is much hate in this world filled with tombstones and graves. Children are being killed and molested, many are orphans! Suicide bombers are killing at will, crimes exist, murder happening daily, homosexuality and prostitution exists and freedom and peace is not globally!

Lucifer was created by God, but Lucifer turned from God and grew evil hating God; he rejected God's way and became Satan; the killer of love and all that God created!

Remember Satan has but a short time, it seems long in human terms but life is like one day to God. Satan knows he will be bound for eternity, dead and gone forever! And this is the fate Satan wants all mankind part of as well. Satan doesn't want mankind to dwell with God and Jesus Christ forever in eternity. Satan does not want mankind to know God, he wants us to reject God and he wants us to sin! Satan doesn't want us to live tomorrow he wants us to die today! Live today for tomorrow we die! This is what Satan wants mankind to live like, a life of sorrow and hate, depression and despair, murder and death, this is what Satan wants us to believe life is about.

Our lives will change! And it will change to holiness the moment we receive God and His Spirit into our lives, the moment we repent to God, when we believe in Him and in Christ Jesus our Lord. Amen.

The moment we receive God in our life we'll have a pro-founding effect on those around us, those who know us. It may be a wonderful fulfillment in their lives as well or they may simply reject you. But let your light so shine before everyone, be an example of our living Lord Jesus Christ and our loving God and be kind and gentle to everyone.

Remember, the glory of God's heaven will be with us and all things will be made new, those you knew will be with you; and the life you longed for will be everlasting. And tomorrow will be the fulfillment of God's love for all His children.

In *Revelation 21:3-5* it reads: and I heard a loud voice from heaven saying, "Behold, the tabernacle of God is with men and He will dwell with them, and they shall be His people and God Himself will be with them and be their God." "And God will wipe away every tear from their eyes; there shall be no more death, sorrow, crying and there shall be no more pain, for the former things have passed away." Then He sat on the throne and said, "Behold, I make all things new."

Tomorrow

Tomorrow is like today, accompanied by Oppression and Violence that never goes away.

Tomorrow awaits the voices of fear, many people will pray; for the sorrows of a lifetime felt in one day.

There's a place that can't be denied, spoke of through our Children, as Christ was by their side, never to run, never to hide; with God we will abide.

Tomorrow is past, Today is a new, all the Knowledge and Promises of God, was taught to you; though I am alive, some never knew.

Today came to pass in a twinkling of an eye, Christ is with you, you 'll never die; this God said is very true, Today you will be with Me in Paradise, and Tomorrow will be new.

Immortality

The Lord looks down from heaven upon the children of men, to see if there are any who understand, who seek God. There is no partiality with God. God gives glory, honor and peace to everyone who works to do what is good. God also gives eternal life to those who by patient continuance in doing good; seek for glory, honor and immortality.

God spoke, and wrote the commandments many years ago. For many scholars and believers it's known as, (The Laws of God), written by his very hand to us His children. Over the course of time, and a time after the laws of God became manifested, through a new covenant God established. With His children it became evident that the Laws and Spirit of God lives and dwells within and through us. To which God gives us, so we to one another as we continue growing in the grace and knowledge of our Lord Jesus Christ.

Show the work of the law not written in books or in stone but written in your heart; be just in the sight of God. Your conscience, also bearing witness and your thoughts accusing or else excusing you in the day when God will judge the secrets of men by Jesus Christ, according to the gospel.

For the many this is a mystery; we shall not all sleep, but we for shall be changed. For this corruptible must put on incorruption and this mortal must put on immortality.

In a moment, in the twinkling of an eye, at the last trumpet the trumpet will sound and the dead will be raised incorruptible and we shall be changed. And, it shall be brought to pass the saying that is written: "Death is swallowed up in Victory." But thanks be to God, who gives us the victory through our Lord Jesus Christ.

Fight the good fight of faith laid hold on eternal life to which you were also called and have confessed the good confession in the presence of many witnesses. And, remember this faithful saying: For if we died with Him, we shall also Live with him. If we endure we shall also reign with Him. If we deny him he will also deny us. If we are faithless, He remains faithful; He cannot deny himself.

Jesus Christ has saved us and called us with a holy calling not according to our works but according to his own purpose and grace which was given to us in Christ Jesus before time began, which has been revealed by the appearing of our Savior Jesus Christ, who has abolished death and brought life and immortality to light through the Gospel.

And so, "Let your light so shine before men, that they may see your good works and glorify your Father in heaven." And, I close with this prayer to our God in heaven; "Your Kingdom come, Your will be done, on earth as it is in heaven. Amen."

Heavenly Lights

We are heavenly lights, growing up angels in a human body; Christ like in every way. And God will set us apart from the mortal life we live, yet it's our choice and decision for He will truly give.

Overcoming temptations, evil and earthly pleasures Strengthens our heart and mind. It takes you closer to heaven, where peace, joy and love replace earthly treasures.

If you're a child of God and heaven is your home, believe that God created you; and your life is not your own.

For we are alien's in a foreign "world, an image of the Creator God, dressed by the grace of His glory; walking in the Lord's foot-shod.

And we are visible yet invisible revealed by Jesus Christ, who brought life and immortality to light, And God's reflection through you, who's kingdom is always in sight, for you are God's blessing, His glorious Heavenly Light.

Freedom, One Unity with God
Written By: Grace E. Richter

We are brothers and sisters in Christ
All Created by the eternal one
So let us join hands around the world for what God
*   has done*
Unity, Praise lets remember His name
He knows all of ours so let's testify and sing
*   together*
(Chorus)
To live to pray is a blessing everyday
To be, in love with the Almighty God Above
You give each day to us
Let's sing, let's praise, for the Freedom we have
*   today*
To hear your voice and not have anyone say
You cannot Pray
God gave our country Freedom
He made the nations
They should have the same rights as you and me
It's better to fight for Freedom and Family
Then to always be chasing for Money and greed

*Almighty Love comes from the Lord above through peace
And harmony
(Back to Chorus)
There are people dying for Freedom today
The freedom to bring them peace
To be able to hold a Bible in their hands and say
I have a choice I can live God's way.
(Back to Chorus)
Waking each day not knowing if you are going to die
Willing to take that chance
For the most Holy God above
To have Freedom and peace for all Eternity
Don't God deserve it for giving us Love
He gave His only begotten Son
We took His Son and just threw Him away
But He still gives us Love and Forgiveness every day
(Back to Chorus)
Don't you think the other Nations have the same right as you and I to call to the Lord Above?
There were planes that fell from the sky the Unity we had that day
Wouldn't it be nice to have a world where unity was everyday
Where you don't need some terrible event reminding you of
"What could be?
So, let's help the other nations to have Peace and Harmony!!!!!!!!!
(Back to Chorus)*

The Spirit

The Spirit, what's it like? Is the spirit like the wind that moves blades of grass? Blows hard against your home knocking against the glass. Does it make the waters move? Or, change the form of clouds. Does it spring forth like flowers after the earth's been plowed?

What's the Spirit Like I wonder? Does it make the sky blue? Can it cause thunder? Does if move winter, spring, autumn, or summer? When it's resisted, can nations plunder?

The Spirit? It's Alive! And, in you it's within. No, it can't be seen, but helps when you sin. The spirit is unlike a dream, it's real like the Lord you have seen. So, remember and keep this in mind; "Turn your heart to the Lord and His Spirit you shall find."

Call to God You All the Earth

Allow me to ask you, 'Will you embark on a Journey with me?" But, first imagine and embrace the wonderful teaching and kindness love of our eternal Father:

God's love has been taught by many people throughout generations over a trillion times over again!

God's mercy has reigned and washed over a multitude of people throughout all generations!

I can go on and on however, I am certain you get the history here. So much of God's love has been taught to us by countless people to instruct and proclaim the Glory of His eternal Gospel, and Life for all mankind. There are many known religions, organizations, churches and groups. The Gospel of the Lord has been widespread throughout the world in numerous ways.

The journey includes the entire race of all mankind. Believe, for the glory of God's people will in one voice, one heart, one love, call out to God in prayer, in steadfast hope and in complete faith. O' God our Father, forgive us our sins we confess before You, no more will we choose false gods or idols, and no more will we deny Your name. We call on You our Lord and Savior receive us into Your life today and forever cleanse our hearts and minds. Sanctity us O' God we love, honor and worship You Father of all creation. Bring forth Your promise among Your people and establish Your name into the hearts of all mankind. For Your will be done on earth as it is in heaven, and give us this day our daily bread and deliver us from the evil one,

"For Yours is the Kingdom the power and glory now and forever!"

Our entire world, all of us need to call out to God, when will we begin?

LaVergne, TN USA
12 May 2010
182510LV00004B/53/P